September, 2017
The 70th ....

D0686321

The Absolute,
Relatively Inaccessible

The Absolute,
Relatively Inaccessible

Walter Wangerin Jr.

Foreword by Scott Cairns

CASCADE *Books* • Eugene, Oregon

THE ABSOLUTE, RELATIVELY INACCESSIBLE

Copyright © 2017 Walter Wangerin Jr. All rights reserved. Except for brief quotations in critical publications or reviews, no part of this book may be reproduced in any manner without prior written permission from the publisher. Write: Permissions, Wipf and Stock Publishers, 199 W. 8th Ave., Suite 3, Eugene, OR 97401.

Cascade Books
An Imprint of Wipf and Stock Publishers
199 W. 8th Ave., Suite 3
Eugene, OR 97401

www.wipfandstock.com

PAPERBACK ISBN: 978-1-5326-1669-3
HARDCOVER ISBN: X978-1-4982-4062-8
EBOOK ISBN: 978-1-4982-4061-1

Cataloguing-in-Publication data:

Names: Wangerin, Walter, author | Cairns, Scott, foreword.

Title: The absolute, relatively inaccessible / Walter Wangerin Jr. ; foreword by Scott Cairns.

Description: Eugene, OR: Cascade Books, 2017.

Identifiers: ISBN 978-1-5326-1669-3 (paperback) | ISBN 978-1-4982-4062-8 (hardcover) | ISBN 978-1-4982-4061-1 (ebook)

Subjects: LCSH: Poetry.

Classification: PS3573 A477. 2017 (paperback) | PS3573 (ebook).

Manufactured in the U.S.A.   05/11/17

Contents

Foreword

When Mystery Matters Most

Over the years, I have received a good many poems from a good many clergy folk who were keen to offer their wisdom in verse form. Most often—nearly always—what they have offered is but a curiously unsatisfying species of sermon. Their slender texts generally manifest little sense of why they were not simply presented in prose, or simply offered from the pulpit of a Sunday morning.

Genuine poems, of course, are not sermons. Nor are they bits of received wisdom pared into narrow shapes of parsed out, line-phrased syntax. Poems are not opportunities for one person to teach another something that he or she has seen fit to share. That is not to say that one doesn't learn a good deal while poring over a genuine poem; the poet herself is the first to do so, in the very midst of shaping the poem at hand.

Poems—if they are truly poems—are best understood as scenes of meaning-making, sites where a poet or a pastor or a pastor-poet has himself trusted language—the agency of the very word—to lead him into seeing and saying what he could not otherwise have seen or said. Tended with care, that site can continue to serve as generative scene for further meaning-making when a duly attentive reader brings her own energies into the chewy linguistic mix.

I begin with these admittedly cranky observations in order to contextualize—as well as to set apart from the commonplace—the exceeding delight and surprise I experienced as I pored over this late book of poetry from Walter Wangerin, a man whose novels, essays, stories, memoirs, and—yes—sermons I have savored for the better part of four decades.

From his first poem (a lyrically charged ekphrastic beauty called "Adams' Photograph of Stieglitz") through intermittent narratives, epistles, meditations, and clear to the last long poem (a brilliant midrash on the Mesopotamian *Poems of Heaven and Hell*, and a bona fide *tour de force*) Wangerin the poet has done what few Christians, few clergy, and few servants of the word ever accomplish; he has set aside our common penchant for easy consolation, favoring a strenuous pursuit of authenticity and truth, wielding as his only tool a tenacious faith that language—its echoing music, its provocative cadences, its taste on the tongue—will lead him into glimpsing otherwise unavailable knowledge. One presumes that such an uncommonly fierce devotion to pressing language for a glimpse of *truth* has come about through Wangerin's serious illness of some ten years.

I think it is fair to say that most of us, most of the time, manage to make it through our middling days with little need to press beyond what we might call *the accessible*, our *paraphrases of truth*. That is to say, if we are blessed with reasonable health and manageable family lives, we can keep at bay the nagging suspicion that *what is* exceeds what we can say or know. We can continue to cling to our familiar *terms* as if they proved a satisfying *terminus*, a likely end of discussion.

That said, suffering has a way of nudging us ahead; the *apparent* becomes insufficient, our knowledge becomes patently unsatisfactory, and we are thereby obliged to reconsider the *terminal* as a new point of departure, the beginning of yet another passage, leaning into *the Absolute*. Thus nudged, the poet has but one way ahead, and that is to press language for revelation.

Walt Wangerin has written that, under such circumstances, "It isn't okay to be bitter." One discovers in these poems, however, that it is okay—even efficacious—to be honest in the darkness, reaching for whatever light the dawn affords. This is when mystery matters most, when we no longer care to be comforted by the partial and the insufficient, but rather risk all such comforts for a finer sense of the Enormity in which we live and move and have our being.

As the voice of his first poem affirms, so too does the poet labor. The poems of this late collection, *The Absolute, Relatively Inaccessible*, manifest both a tribute and a legacy

> whereby each man defines,
> each man revises
> the dark and the daylight.

One revises in order to see, and to see again, and to see truly, ever so.

—Scott Cairns

Adams' Photograph of Stieglitz

In 1939 Ansel Adams photographed the photographer Alfred
Stieglitz while the latter stood in an indiscernible corner
of his gallery, An American Place.

Your praise is never disintegrating … I can see only one thing to do—make
photography as clean, as decisive, and as honest as possible.

Adams' letter to Stieglitz, November 1963

1.

So white
the twice-high ceiling
and white the walls that stand background
to the old man's figure;

so white the corner-join behind him
it scarcely makes a shadow.
Existence purified, you might say—
except for this one dark thing,

Alfred Stieglitz, whose right hand
hangs slack at his waist,
holding the stem of his eyeglasses
loosely between his fingers.

The old photographer wears a black
double-breasted suit:
a buttoned vest, rumpled pants,
and a white, open-collared shirt.

But his slouch (which discomposes the hang of the jacket)
and his insouciance (one jacket-flap fully in its pocket,
the other, one corner in, one corner out)
belie the suit's formality.

Alfred's eyes are as distant as white-noise,
the lip-edge of his moustache
sheared as straight
as a technical principle.

2.

Most folks know Ansel Adams as a photographer
in awe-full communion with the violent moon,
that argent globe fixed in midnight,
indifferent to the wrack of cenotaphs below.

Most ought to know Stieglitz as the first to claim place
for black-and-white photographs
(art, if you please) on the walls of empurpled museums—
MoMA of the muses;

and most *ought* to know him as a paterfamilias
in communion with young initiates
like this broad-faced Adams fresh from the west,
whose photos Stieglitz displayed on the walls of his "American
Place."

3.

Ansel's camera, its flash, his shot of Alfred
(the whole pictorial act)
counts two segments
in the unbroken helix
that spirals back
through countless generations of artists—
back to the gloaming wherein God said, *Light!*

Ansel's photograph and his mentor
(black against white walls)
is a tribute (craft for craft)
and a legacy (eyes for eyes)
whereby each man defines,
each man revises
the dark and the daylight.

Part 1

Snow

Cones of Snow

1. The Evening Vigil

They've sewn Odessa's eyelids
closed,
the lashes the stitching.

The old mortician tried for a smile,
but settled for an inane
twist of her lips.

Once as black and as rich
as a grand-black piano,
Odessa's complexion's stained sallow;

eyeglasses askew
on the bridge of her nose
What? The woman wore glasses?

There's a knoll in Oakhill Cemetery,
fenced to define the plots
reserved for Negroes.

2. Graveside, Afternoon

Rev Leroy and I stand alone
beside the open hole:
"Earth. Ashes. Dust."

The Rev snaps closed his Bible
and quits the canvas canopy
billowing in the wintry wind.

Two white groundskeepers
unwinch the casket down:
ta-tocka ta-tocka, ta-tocka—

"Hurry up, Joe!
I'm frost-bit!"

3. Dusk

I drive home under the streetlamps
that swing from crossed wires
above the intersections.

The light of a single streetlamp
forms in the air before me
a ghostly cone of snow,

the cone's low circle
of fallen light
lying on a loose inch of snow.

4. Noonday

A warm Indian-summer sun
melts the snow that last night
mounded Miz Odessa's tomb,

dissolves the headstone
that should have stood memorial
to the woman's weary life.

Milk and Snow in Three Declensions

1.

The December snows muffle the sounds of human vowels.
The sibilant ice cracks the distance like a rifle shot.

2.

Before we can see the horse-drawn milk wagon
laboring uphill
("I'll see it first!"
"Look out for me, Wally,
cause *I'm* gonna see it first!!")

Before the mare pulls
the metal, butter-colored wagon
around the corner to our street,
we children can hear the kindly,
congregational clinking of its bottles.

Here she comes,
dobbin slow-plodding,
uncomplaining,
blinkered and blanketed,
nodding with every fore-step down
on the packed snow,
with every maul-hoof down.

Then here comes the milkman
bustling up the neighbor's walk—
six bottles in a wire basket—
both he and the mare discharging steam:
his a fume from his nostrils,
hers a twinning of gun-puffs.

In those days the bottles
bulged at their necks,
separating the mellow cream
from the serous milk below.

We knock on the windowpane,
("Mares-y doats, and does-y doats. . . .")
We knock, then dash out into an air so cold
it clicks my wet hair hard as a carapace—

do dash out the front door
to rush the bottles back inside
before the bottle lifts its cardboard hat
on an ice-cream column.

Politely:
"How do you do?"
"Fine, Mr. Cream,
and how are you?"

The mare progresses like a river-barge
between banks of seven-foot snows
piled on either side of our Canadian street—
snow-castles we will be kings of tomorrow.

3.

Cattle, wintering on the Canadian plains,
turn their rumps to the blizzard's fusillade,

their heads adroop
as if let down on ropes.

All night the beasts breathe forth frost.
By dawn their muzzles are frozen
by blunt columns of ice
to the solid, unforgiving ground.

O you monuments of patience,
bowed and locked to the iron earth,
and waiting to perish—
must you die still standing up?

4.

Now here's this other mare
who's lost her footing
and gone walloping down into the pit
my neighbor bulldozed
and cinder-blocked last autumn
to build the foundation
on which, come spring,
he plans to build a house.

The mare lies on her side
on dirty ice like a tractor-trailer,
throwing up her head as a counterweight
for heaving her body up again.

My children hear the mare's pained neighing.
They rush from of the house, crying,
"Bell! Bell! O Bell!"
then, turning to the back door, crying,
"Daddy! Anabelle's hurt!"

I, too, dash outside.
Bell's cannon-bone has been broken,
a sharp piece of bone
piercing through the flesh.

I pound on my neighbor's trailer house.
"Ezra!" crying, "Bell's broken a leg!"
And to my children,
"Go inside!"

But the mare's lip
lifted above her yellow teeth,
and her eyes,
rolling white and wild—

Jesus *Christ!*
What child can abandon the awful?
Heroes don't
lie down
and die.

My neighbor steps out.
He crosses the snow
carrying in the crook of his arm
his .257 Weatherby

Bell's flank steams.
Her head hits down
with the dead-thump
sacks of wheatmeal make.

Her forelock whips the filthy ice,
her blood inscribing
indecipherable cuneiform words.

5.

Winter's vowels
cannot communicate.
But the rifle shot
cracks the cosmos.

A Torque of Time

1.

In something like a flash of rapture
lightning leaps
through Miz Margaret Denne's keyhole,

scorches the varnish on her tea-table,
and scores the hardwood floor
with a linear scrawl: *Haphazard.*

Lightning impacts
Miz Denne's chest,
leaving behind a lazy electrical smoke.

2.

Nature x-rays
the small bones
in the old woman's wrist,

scrolls the air with cinder-smoke,
demonstrating in a torque of time
that all her creeds have keyholes.

Gertrude's Letter, Midwinter

Tell the truth, I wondered if you might not come.
The uncertain snows, of course,
and the time it takes to drive
from Saskatoon to Bismarck here—
traveling between the needs, so to speak.

But your letter answered, and I am. . . .
Well, you've a handsome mind, Dylan,
and a liquid run of language. . . .
I am . . .
resolved.

I'll salt the walks and
shovel the wet-heavy snow from the roof and
cut back the furnace and
pull the drapes and
keep the parlor closed
against the North Dakota cold.

It's a pretty question, isn't it,
which is your home?—
the American bedroom furnished
with a length-wise love for you,
or that carbolic necessity
lying to north in Canada,

lying on the bed of your birthing
and the breasts of your nursing
and the farmland fallow far too long
and a winter for which there will be no spring.

Neither one, I suppose, there being two.
You're called upon to be just where you are,
and thought upon, not being here.

You wrote you couldn't come.
I have the letter at my elbow.
You laid in decorous lines your explanation:
A thousand obligations try
if I can't go by bits insane.

You wrote how fever has rouged
the brace of your mother's cheekbones,
and deeper still that deliberate scar,
and you, her only child.

Darling, inscribed on your watermarked paper,
Darling, as if we lay in bed together,
your murmur a trouble of pebbles
made music under a summer's brook:
My darling, my fair, my lovely Mrs. Thomas,
it's the dying that demands me.
Mother has clutched her terminus—
"Terminus," Dylan?
—and shawled a piece of death
around her shoulders. . . .
Dylan, Dylan,
What knots of language.

Indigo, indigo, indigo blue,
here is my letter back to you—

how I have resolved this,
my indifferent winter.

One cannot turn from a terminal thing
to the thing you've called *perdurable*.
Cannot turn from the scrolling frost
of her exhalations
to the more certain
(how would you say it?)
insufflations here.

Or call it the snows.
Say it's the weather.
I'll keep the parlor closed.
Tell your mother.

Miz Lillian's Memorial Stones

1. October

Douglas—a ginger-stick of a little man,
his head a cheerful filbert,
his mouth a pouch of repeatable phrases—
Douglas Lander never learned to drive a car.

It was his custom to walk the city's grid,
pausing at street corners
palavering with old friends
until the evening pulled her shade.

The Landers,
Douglas and Lillian
(his wife primevally)
together wore the mantle of Elijah.

They were as common as pepper shakers
on a kitchen table—
unremarkable fixtures in the inner city,
making the mean streets neighborly.

Douglas could recall
the histories of the inner city,
granting the past a present life.

"Was a time" he'd say,
"when Line Street *was* a line,
black folk to east, white folk to west,
nor never a man to cross,
'less bid-ness tuck him over.

"Nowadays we blacks on *bof* sides.
One 'o them thangs," he said,
smiling pleasantly,
his eyes merry behind glasses
over-large and silver-stemmed.
"One o' them thangs."

The Landers were the watch-wards
of the neighborhood.

For their sakes
do not call it a ghetto.
Do not presume it to be
a warren of squalor.

Douglas and Lillian were
the Hassidic "Laméd Vavniki,"
the Righteous Ones on whose account
God does not destroy the universe.

2. December

Miz Lillian sits in her rocking chair.
Douglas, give me this bit of a minute.
Soon I'm gon' rise up an' kiss you,
kiss you, Douglas, gone and goodbye.

While carrying
a slice of pecan pie and a fork on a plate
carrying them from the kitchen

to Lawrence Welk in the parlor,
Douglas collapsed.
His silver-stemmed glasses spun across the floor
and fetched up between his wife's feet.

Crick, crick—
the sound of her rocking.
Aloud Miz Lil says, "You allus did come home
wif milk or some such other I sent you for."

Lillian's slippers are like bandages
on her swollen feet.
Though she's but a nickel's worth of weight,
it pains her to stand on them.

Lillian kisses her husband,
gone and goodbye.

    3. The New Year

The vigil.
The casket set on two sawhorses
in the parlor.

Then the funeral.
Then the headstone,
and then the snowfall.

Except for her daughters' cheer-me-up
chatter,
the tinseled tree,
carols and fruitcakes,
Lilian's Christmas
passes undisturbed.

    4. The Diamond-Jeweled Night

A full moon descends the dark
outside Miz Lander's window
when the preacher steps
into her shadowed parlor.

Miz Lil says,
"Rest your coat."

Crick, crick. Crick, crick,
the runners of her rocking chair
on the hardwood floor.

"Cup o' coffee?"
"No, thank you.
Wouldn't be able to sleep tonight."

Swoosh, swoosh—
a different, softer sound,
Lillian caressing her stomach
under its gingham shirt.

"The pain of his passing," she says.
"Ah'm full used to it by now."

A handkerchief of moonlight
slides Lillian-ward across the floor.

"It a gravestone," she murmurs,
"in Oakhill Cemet'ry
where my girls go to grieve.
It a different stone in me."

"A glass o' wine? No?
A slice o' pie? No?"

That patch of moonlight
reaches Lillian's slippers
then rises slowly to her knees,
then on her gingham shirt.

Miz Lil stops rocking.
She muses on some thought
deeper than the preacher can comprehend.

Finally the moon illumines her face
where ancient wrinkles have inscribed
the primordial histories
of humankind.

Lillian says that the stone in her womb
is Douglas,
the widow's unbirthable child.
"Keeps me company," she murmurs.
"Ah've come ret fond of it."

Crick.

Et in Pacem

Watching, last night,
the soft fall of snow
outside his bedroom window,
my old, bewhiskered grandfather
smiled,
one yellow tooth in his head.

Part 2

Cancer

I. On an Age-Old Anvil, Wince and Sing

Does life assert,
remanding death
to the earth beneath her skirts?
Does life expand to fill
the infinities she becomes?

Or is death the void
defining galaxies
as drumbeats define the silences?
Is death the air that shapes
the thing that is not there?

Is life *das Ding an sich*
and grace her growing?

Or death all space
and dying his disrobing?

II. Pain

1.

I shit swamps.

My throat's a coal chute,
my stomach a scuttle.
Marsh-bog crams the sausage casings
of my bowels.

I contain pain.

2.

Pain whizzes
the roots of my hair.

Pain is a hawthorn sapling
growing in my gut.

3.

Pain is larval,
worming the pith of my sacral bone,
causing so sick-sweet a titillation

I want to clobber my goddam sacrum
until it becomes the ache
I comprehend.

4.

Groaning helps.
Swearing helps.
I recommend them.

III. November

1.

Snowflakes feather the air,
dimensioning the air
above the farmer's field—

in the distance
falling slowly,
patiently;

closer, falling swiftly,
alarmingly,
threatening isolation.

2.

Long, corduroy swaths,
the plowed fields
stretch to the horizon,
the snow-furrows white,
the ridgelines black.

IV. The Wanderer

I am the World-Rim-Walker.
I tread the sheer crags
where night and daylight
contour one another.

V. The better metaphor

1.

Mr. TV Anchor maunders to his millions:
"After a heroic battle with cancer, he—"
 (what? Triumphed?)
"—died."
(Isn't that always the way?)
"Our thoughts and prayers go out to . . . ."
(To what? The air?)
As I said, a vapid,
meaningless maundering.

The tone of the oncologist
makes weapons of therapies.
　　Quick boys!
　　Gas that cancer!
　　Irradiate the criminal tissue!
(To what end,
if not to die another day?)

2.

But cancer needn't be an assassin
to be battled but never defeated.

I have the better metaphor:
cancer opens fresh adventures
to experiences
I've never known before.

I am Eric, sailing the western seas,
brine stinging my face,
salt-wind cross-hatching my sunburned face,
alerting me to the self
within my self's delimiting skin.

Pain is the longboat
from which I map
the ragged shoreline
of my New World.

Dying, yes,
but undefeated.
Triumphant!

I, the World-Rim-Walker,
stride continents
before I slip into the sea.

VI. Advice

1.

"Rush through your
bucket-list, boy!"

2.

"Cast Satan out of you!
Pray Jesus to damn the cancer to hell!"

3.

"Meditation. Yoga.
Acupuncture."

4.

"There's this doctor I know
down old Mexico way."

5.

"Slurries of cat's claw, Walt.
Turmeric in warm milk."

6.

"Flights of angels
wing thee to thy rest."

7.

None of these
address my calamity,

reveal, rather,
the cancers of their characters.

VII. Endnote

Save this file,
or delete it—
What I mean's defile it.
It's all the same to me.

VIII. Zero at the Bone

1. Humor

So cold this winter,
I shiver in bed.
Yet sweat sops my sheets.

The tusked grotesque leers at me,
sitting on my chest so heavily
I can't breathe.

"I'm under the weather, ha ha."
Hell. Forgive a sick man's sick effort
at humor.

2. Windstorm

Hail ticks my windowpanes.
Winter bullets
my bedroom window.

"Window," we say,
ignorant that the root of the word
is the ancient Norse "Wind Eye."

A fusillade of hailstones!
Winter's voice is the howling
of his wind.

3. Winter says:

In the gall of my violent nights
I turn the sick man's yearnings
into fog.

My breath shreds the fog.
My breathing blasts his spirit
ragged.

I am the popping trees.
I am the snowblind.
I am the frost that freezes eyes.

I swoop from the Ice-Giant down,
from the polar regions
down.

4. Winter says:

The eye-streaks of the nine-killer shrike
are black,
her beak a Barbary hook.

She impales
living grasshoppers
on hawthorn spikes,

and mice, alive,
on barbs
to keep her meals fresh.

My eye-streaks—
my bristling brows—
are white.

I have spiked the sick man
on the ice-hooks of my seeing.
I've pinned his lungs to a post.

Ice survives
till a cold man
dies.

Gash my glittering back!—
and I will hoar forth
blizzards.

Mount the white foam of my roaring!—
and I will bridle
the clouds.

I've locked the man's knuckles.
Have chapped his lips.
Have cracked his teeth speechless.

I am sleet
against the sick man's
face.

My teeth snaggle-freeze
the water at the rims
of lakes.

My skull encases
the white
horizons.

In my season, all is mine.
What abides
is mine.

Death
can't kill
death.

IX. Slow time

1. The waters

Once Time, like a vehement stream,
rushed tumultuous down the mountain-rocks;

now Time lies like a broad water
two inches deep.

I walk the water, closely observing,
since Time grants me time before The Time.

2. The fields

Wild Apple blossoms release
a companionable bridal fragrance.

Honeysuckles breathe forth
a lascivious scent.

Tulips are cups
awaiting wine.

The Wild Strawberry flaunts her sun-yellow breast
wreathed in five petals white.

Redbuds are
earth's auroral sigh.

Lilacs in Victorian dress,
exude a workaday redolence.

3.

Eve walks Eden, pregnant
with seeds of living stars.

X. Time's Gyre

Cancer collapses Time,
turning this present moment
into the spool around which
all Time is winding—
and I abide in the axial
vortex of eternity.

XI. Necrophagia:
The Mastery of the Thing

When she digs,
she makes a ticking sound
which clocks the passage of Time
(the topic no man can dispute).

Char-black, thumb-thick,
the Burying Beetle digs graves for corpses,
digs down through duff and soil
and (why not?) ice and stone.

Tick-ticking toils,
unrushed, unvaried, cowled in a decent reverence
which nonetheless does not disturb her duty
or hinders her tweezy *pick-picking* down.

Why should I consider her internment
more inglorious
than that with a Bible
in a Lutheran churchyard?

XII. The Effects of Radiation

Plowman, harrow my hair.
Reap my eyebrows.

Harvest the bushes in my nostrils.
Store my pubic patch in barns.

Render my person as naked
as a Christmas goose.

XIII. To Those I Haven't Time to Write

1.

Winter's tree has nothing to say.
    Apply in spring.
    Await the green tongue
of the elm's unfolding leaf.

2.

Summer susurrates a redundance of sibilants—
    the aspen's quivering,
    the cottonwood's rustling
in the speechless breezes.

3.

Accept the round vowel O
    of autumn's apple.
    Ask by the readiness.

4.

Attend to the bells of the redwood's rings.
    Expect one word
to last four seasons long.

XIV.

Remind me.
Remind
me, remind me of crickets
chirping in a moonlit wood.

XV.

(...)

Part 3

O Babylon!

From the Mesopotamian
Poems of Heaven and Hell

I. From *The Babylonian Creation*

1.

Seven days, O Bel-Marduk,
Will I sing.
Through seven days
I will chant your rituals,
worshipping in your lapis lazuli temple.

In the month of Nisan,
will I cry the rites
of Time before
the creation of times.

Such is my service.
Such is my duty.

2.

While neither Height nor Depth
nor Path nor Place existed,

nor yet Names nor Gods
(for gods can become and be
only at the soundings of their names)
there exists Day
before the creation of days.

There exists Apsu,
the Sweet-Water Abyss,
he alone.

Then, in Time
before the times,
there swells a great sea-being,
unwept and unweeping,
an ocean-breaker heaving up,
the Salt-Bitter Tiamat.

In the World
before worlds,
the Sweet-Water Abyss
and the Embittered Ocean-Surge
commingle.

In the Month
before there are months,
countless gods bulk and struggle
in Tiamat's womb
their turgid strife
distending her baby-chamber.

Tiamat labors.
Tiamat delivers
two swarms of bee-like gods,
those that sting and those
that gather honey.

To the gods he will not love,
Apsu gives names
of envenomed thorns.

To the gods he will surely love,
Apsu gives names
of nectars.

In the Year
before years,
and Air
before air,
Apsu comes to despise
the stingings and the whinings
of Tiamat's spiteful brood.

He swears an oath:
"My hand on high," he says,
"I will destroy them
every one!"

By the voice of her sea-crashings
Tiamat swears an oath:
"I bore them. They are *mine*.
My hand on high,
before you drown my children
I will consume yours,
every one!"

There follows, then, a millennial strife,
powers against powers contending;
waterspouts, bitter and sweet,
tornados and typhoons rising gigantic,
causing the cosmos to quake.

3.

Now, upon Apsu's foam,
a boy is born,
a boy-god whom his father names
Marduk,
declaring, "My son's warrings
will outmatch the wars
of Tiamat's children,
and the rages
of Tiamat!"

The infant Marduk
sucks the paps of goddesses.

Then, in the Year
before years,
the man-god Marduk becomes the pride
of his father.

Apsu cries, "Oh, what majesty!
Oh, his radiant stride!"

Marduk's eyes
see as four eyes see—
beyond the infinities.

Marduk's ears
hear as four ears hear—
the clicks of a cricket's dream.

4.

Tiamat—that vinegar hag—
now breeds a new brood.
She spawns

the serpent with caliper fangs,
spawns the dragon
encrusted with jeweled scales
like the jewels of a god-like glory.

Tiamat breeds and births
marsh-maggots,
the two-titted kraken,
the she-lion,
the mad whelp,
and the man-scorpion.

She suckles
the whirling tempests.

Apsu's nectar-gods assemble
to take counsel together.
They say, "The muscled coil of Tiamat
is too fathomless for us.

Apsu!" they cry.
"Send us your son!"

Marduk appears,
his presence his only word.

The honey-gods
beg of him salvation.

"We are too scant
to confound great Tiamat.

O Bel-Marduk, it must be *your* task.
You, the courageous;
you, built like the bull;
you, sceptered with the golden mace;

you, weaponed with the four-furlong spear;
you, bequeathed by your father
the net woven of his own ten thousand hairs."

Bel-Marduk says,
"Even so."
He says
"Even so."

Shamash, Sword of the Sun, hisses,
"Slit her bitter throat!"
Adad, God of Storms, roars,
"Blow her blood-spume
into the bottomless!"

Then, in the War
before wars,
Marduk yokes four mane-flaming coursers
to the chariot he has formed of clouds.

Electric!—is the speed of his flight!
Strobe-lightning forks his face!
War-pennants, war-banners
are Marduk's his wild hair,
snapping in the universe!

Tiamat coils.
She slits her eyes at the hero's
sky-flying down.

Marduk is stars descending.
Marduk is constellations,
Orion, the mighty hunter,
Canis Major, descending.
Aas Pegasus
Bel-Marduk quits his chariot.

Tiamat spits defiance.
The jeweled dragon hisses venom.
The man-scorpion loops his tail forward,
unsheathing his stinging stiletto.

Marduk drops.
He whirls his father's net.
He casts the ten thousand hairs,
entangling Tiamat's
yelping brood.

Tiamat counters.
She spreads wide her thighs.
The lips of her vulva
utter maledictions
She opens her vagina
as wide as a cavern
to swallow the man-god down.

Bel-Marduk, rider of tornados,
blasts breath in Tiamat's womb.
Bloats the womb of Tiamat.
With the blade of his four-furlong spear
pierces Tiamat's baby-chamber.

Her brood issues stillborn on the ground:
dead maggots flowing like an ivory waterfall;
the man-scorpion's stiletto poisonless;
the she-lion and the two-titted kraken
knotted in the ropes
of the mad whelp's bowels.

Marduk's golden mace
cracks Tiamat's skull.
He thumb-pops her eyeballs out,
hurls them into the midnight sky—
the old moon with the new moon in her arm.

Of her brains the Creator forms the soil;
of her joints, the mountains;
of her saliva, rivers;
of her hip-bones, the arcs of the firmament;
of her blood, fountains
with which the Vegetable King
shall water his groves
and irrigate his gardens.

Now—Time
after the times,
and World
after worlds—
creation is complete.

5.

I purify your temple, O Bel-Marduk.
I sanctify its lapis lazuli sanctuary with kettledrums,
and by burning the oils of balm in your silver censors,
the scent of cypress-wood a smoke of jasmine
blown up into your nostrils.

Such is my duty.
Such is my service.

II. From *The Hymn of the Names of Marduk*

1.

Bel-Marduk is One—
Son of the Sun,
the First, the Sunburst.

2.

Bel-Marduk is Russet Wheatfields,
the Harvest he carts to His new-built barns,
the Fan that winnows his foes.

3.

The gods sail safely
on Marduk's blood-fires,
crying acclamations.

4.

Marduk!
Who sows Life
in the Deserts of Death.

5.

Marduk!
Who created humanity
as drone-slaves for the gods.

6.

Woe and weal
is Bel-Marduk.

Sickle and Savior
is He.

7.

Now lift your voices!
Cry to the King of the Green Grass,
"Power!"

Raise your praises in His palace;
raise laudations in His temple.
Time abides after
the ends of times.

III. From *A Prayer to the Gods of Night*

1.

Now is the hour when birds cease stirring;
the hour when stars swing exceedingly low;
the hour to lie on your back like a shepherd
and look.

2.

The palace bars have dropped in their brackets,
the house-bolts shot,
the gates of Babylon
locked.

Great
are the gods
that compose themselves
this night.

The god Shamash,
the god Sin,
and the goddess Inanna
have entered their lofty chambers.

Sight cannot see,
nor can hearing hear
the wanderer
beseeching his god.

Drowsiness covers the fields.
Sleep cloaks the pathways
and the cities
and the temples.

O Shamash, Judge of Truth,
O Enlil, God of the Cosmic Air,
O Ea, Wise in the Ways of Every Art,
abide by me.

IV. From *Childbirth*

1. The Birth-Witch

When the reeds of your basket
stretch and creak,
when your basket bulks with unknown fruit,
O thou laboring woman,
weave an image, warp and woof.
Carve in cedar the likeness
of the demon Lamashtu.

Carve her head like the heads of swine,
her teeth like the teeth of goats,
and her fingers like the talons of raptor birds.

Weave Lamashtu's breasts naked
and as flat as socks,
her nipples like knobs,
one nipple suckling a piglet,
the other suckling a pup.

For she it is, the demon Lamashtu,
who slips softly, softly,
into the birthing room,
seven times stroking a pregnant belly
while chanting the seven spells
of stillbirth and miscarriage.

But listen, O laboring mother:
Lamashtu's witchery can be aborted!

For as much as she terrifies you,
so much more is Lamashtu terrified
by the sight of *herself*.

2. Labor

Woman, the pain of your contractions
bodes a difficult birth.
The bands of your abdomen cry,
"O Marduk,
mercy me!"

Pain cries,
"Snip the threads
that have sewn my child
inside my womb!"

The midwife shuffles to her duties,
pours olive oil on your round mountain,
massages the summit of your womb
until her flesh and your flesh
share the self-same warmth.

Pestle:
the midwife grinds dry fennel seeds.
Mortar:
grinds into a powder.
Then stirs the powder
in a cup of warm, honeyed wine.

"Drink, child.
The draught will ease the straps
of your contractions."

You raise a red streak of screaming.
It's time, now. It is time.

3. Birth

The midwife crouches on a three-legged stool
her hands between your thighs.
"Once more, child.
One more push."

Your hair sticks to the sweat of your brow.
Your lips curl back in a wolf's savage grin.
You lean forward.
You grab your knees
and throttle the wailing within you.

Suddenly the infant slurps
into the cold, mortal world.

"A boy!" the midwife laughs.
Your baby is a boy!"

4. Stillborn

Not so happy the issue
of this mother's second labor.

She thrashes on her bed.
She sweats a salty water.
Flies buzz her face.
Flies sip at the tears in her eyes.

"Oh, my unborn babe!"
the mother cries.
"Why?" she cries.
"Why are you like a bark
heaved up on the foam of the seas?"

Where is Bel-Marduk now?
Where is he?
In a far-off land
accepting honors.
Honors which, he assures himself
are his due.

The mother cries,
"O my child, my child,
what evil has set you adrift?
Who has cut your mooring-rope?"

Where is Inanna now?
Where is she?
Pacing the peaks of her mountain.
Contemplating a leap into hell.

A crushing contraction
throws the mother to the floor.
How taxing the struggle on her knees!
She buries her pleas in her pillow.

The day I suckled my firstborn child,
how happy was my heart,
how happy, my husband and I.

Not Marduk.
Not the Goddess Inanna,
it is Lamashtu who has come
into the bedroom.
It is she who cut the mooring ropes
of the unborn infant.
Seven times around the mother,
seven spells reciting.

The husband wrings his hands.
"Ishtar," he prays.
"O Ereshkigal, Queen of the Great Below,
why sever my wife from me?—
she whose breath once sparkled?"

The mother who delivers the babe on her knees,
cannot see that its lips are blue.
nor that its fingernails are blue.

"No use," the father weeps,
cradling his stillborn daughter
cradled in the crook of his arm.
"No use to tug at the breast
that gives no milk."

"No good, my wife," he wails.
"No good to strain for the breath
that is not there."

The widower sighs.
"There is no good,
no good in the dark winds
of the cosmos."

V. From *Inanna's Journey into Hell*

1.

Inanna's yearning servant asks,
"Why choose the fell road to hell?"
Ninshubar pleads with his mistress,
"Why descend to your sister, Ereskigal,
Queen of the Dark Below?"

From the summit of her mountain
Inanna gazes down,
down,
and yet, again,
down.

"Why?" Ninshubar begs,
"abandon your husband, Dumuzi,
the Fair Son of Truth,
and the shepherd-melodies he pipes?"

Inanna prepares herself.
She shoes her feet with the seven signs of dominion.
She takes up the symbol-reeds of status,
takes up the lapis lazuli measuring rod.

Inanna crowns herself with the wilderness,
robes herself in the gown of sovereignty,
pins to each of her breasts
a perfect, polished oval of onyx,
and shadows her eyes with antimony.

Inanna, listen!
Dead spirits gibber in the black abyss,
fluttering their bat-like wings
through the corridors of hell.

Inanna assures her resurrection
by binding her servant to an oath.
"If I linger too long in my sister's pit,
plead before the doors of the gods,
saying, 'Let not your daughter die in hell!'"

She steps on the viewless air.
Her gown billows like a linen bell.

2.

Count he halls of hell.
They are seven,
their locked gates seven,
opened only for the dead.

Inanna strides to the first gate.
"Neti!" she calls.
"Gatekeeper! Throw back this bolt!"

Bandy-legged Neti peers through the bars.
"So,' he says, "the Blush of Dawn
wishes to benight herself in the Dark Pit
whence none living can return."

"But I have come," Inanna says.
"I have come to attend the funeral rites,"
Inanna lies,
"of Irra, Lord of the Underworld."

Neti raises an eyebrow.
"Know this, that I have
neither the power nor the authority
to grant your blasphemous request.
But!
I will carry your request
to the Mistress of the Assizes,
the awful Queen of Hell."

Inanna, Goddess of the Mountain
has little grace
and less patience.

She may be noble,
but hers is a disdainful nobility.
She hates to wait.

"Well," says Neti at his return,
"your sister has her own designs.
She grants you entrance,
but not without a fee."

"Less and little," says Inanna."

"Doff the shoes of the seven insignia."

"Lesser," says Inanna. "Little."
Barefoot, then, she strides
into the first hall of hell.

In order for Inanna
to enter the second,
the lower hall of hell,
Queen Ereshkigal demands
second forfeiture.

"The symbol-reeds of status," Neti says.
"The lapis lazuli measuring rod."

Not so easy to relinquish signs
of Inanna's authority.

At the third, the gate lower than the second,
Neti demands Inanna's wilderness-crown.

At the fourth gate
demands that she pluck the onyx ovals
from her breasts.

At the fifth:
"The ornaments that have made
uncomeliness comely."

And the sixth:
"Scrub the antimony
from your eyes.
Make plain the face
and lashless the eyes
that mimic beauty."

Finally, at the seventh gate
of the last and the lowest hall of hell,
Neti charges Inanna
to make her greatest sacrifice:

"Strip!" says the gatekeeper.
Denude yourself of your robe"—
in whose weave
is Inanna's identity.

    3.

Naked,
unshod, uncrowned,
unlovely, and unnamed,
Inanna treads hell's cold pavement
to confront that Dark Personage,
the Queen Ereshkigal
seated on her sable throne.

Inanna hones to her own design.
which is to reign in the mountains above
and the nether world below.

"Sweet sister," she begins.
"I have always held in high esteem.
I—"
Ereshkigal interrupts.

"Ye demon-leaches!" she cries.
"Ye Galli!
Hook False-Heart
on hell-pit's iron spike!
Let her swing
like the carcass of a cow!"

    4.

Three days and three nights pass.
Cords of anxiety have tightened
Ninshubar's soul.

He goes to the city Nippur
clothed in beggars' patched.
He lacerates his lips
and stands outside the doors
of the Wind-God's palace.

"Father Enlil!" he calls,
"surely you will not let your daughter's bones
be ground between the hell-stones,
or let her dust be packed
in a boxwood casket."

The Wind-God sweeps answers
with a blast of contempt.
"She chose hell.
No one forced her.
The woman has bound herself
to every law of the Pit!"

Next, before the palace of Anunnak,
God of the Black Plow,
Inanna's servant makes the same plea,
"Surely—"
Savage, the answer of Anunnak.

To Kingu, then,
to Sag-Kal, to Kulili,
to gods and goddesses,
always heaped with scorn.

Last of all Ninshubar
limps on bleeding feet
to the palace of the Wisdom-God,
Ea.

"Father," he wails,
"surely *thou* shalt not
allow thy daughter die
on hell's iron spike."

Great Ea emerges from his palace.
"Inanna, I am grieved," he says.
"O hapless Inanna,
so much grief."

Ninshubar repeats,
"So much grief."

Ea ponders.
He turns his shaggy head
this way and that,
then plucks a thorn from an acacia tree.
With this thorn, Ea digs the dirt
under the cuticle of his lacquered fingernail.

"There is," he murmurs,
"a way."

"A means, Lord Ea?
A solution?"

Of his fingernail clay
the God of Wisdom
forms a man.
He breathes on it,
thereby bringing Kurgarru to life,
one who is neither a man nor a woman.

Ea offers Kurgarru a bit of bread.
"Eat this," he says.
"It is the bread of the living."

Ea pours a cup of wine.
"Drink this.
It is the wine of the living.

Now go, Kurgarru.
Descend.
Swarm the halls of hell.
Buzz like clouds of blowflies.

But have a care that you do not eat
the bread baked in Ereshkigal's
oven of spite,
nor drink the wine
fermented in Ereshkigal's casks of violence.

Say these words to her:
'Release your sister,
Inanna of the mountains."

5.

By morbid paths
and through the seven open gates,
Kurgarru descends
into the seventh hall
of Queen of the Abyss.

Inanna hangs,
hooked on hell's spike,
as naked as a pitcher.

Kurgarru—neither a man,
but with the force of a man,
nor a woman,
but with the sagacity of a woman—
demands of Ereshkigal,

"Release your sister,
she whose realm is a mountain!"

The Pit-Queen blows dust
and shrieks, "Who vexes my bowels?
If a god, then bless you.
If a mortal, then swear by heaven and earth!"

Kurgarru swears by heaven and earth:
"I," he says, "ask nothing, Queen,
but to kiss your sister."

Host of dead spirits
flutter on leather wings,
gibbering like bats.

Kurgarru breathes
swarms of blowflies abroad,
confounding the squeaks
and the flights of the spirit-bats.

The Queen of the Black Rocks
waves a dismissing hand.
"As to your request, why not?
Why not kiss ice
and freeze your lips?"

Kugarru approaches Inanna.
With his kiss
he squirts
the wine of the living into her mouth.
On his tongue is a bite
of the bread of the living.

Inanna's cheeks recover their blush.
Her tears wash her dusty eyes white.
"Deliver me."

Kugarru says,
"I have been formed for this.
I have come to set your free."

He wraps his arm around Inanna's waist
and raises her
from hell's ice-spike.

Ereshkigal shrieks, "No!"
Her cry cracks the cavern walls.
Then she conceives a cunning exchange.

"No one escapes alive—
not unless she replaces her life
with another's life,
one finer than hers."

6.

Inanna is coming!
Inanna is coming up!
Dressed and crowned and shod, is she!
The Galli-leaches cling, writhing,
attached to her skin.

Behold! Inanna *has* come up!

The Galli hiss,
"Whose life, Inanna?
Whose life,
that you may live?"

At a cross-roads stands Dumuzi,
slender-fingered,
piping meadow-music for his wife, Inanna,
the winsome melodies of shepherds.

The Galli squirm.
"Is this the one?"

Inanna narrows her eye
and assesses her husband.
With the eyes of the assizes
she takes Dumuzi's measure,

"Yes," she says.
"This is he.
Take him."

The wild Galli fly at Dumuzi.
They snatch his pipe.
They coil around it
and snap it into five pieces.

"O Shamash!" Dumuzi cries.
"O God of Justice!
Who else milked the ewes,
but I?
Who else brought the cream to your mother,
but I?

Shamash! Transform me!
Cloak my bones in bark!
Thrust my legs deep underground.
Turn my toes into such roots
as no devil can weed me out."

But Shamash is traveling

with the sleeping sun
under the disc of earth,
traveling the night
from the western shores
to the eastern seas.

Dumuzi, Dumuzi,
so much grief.
It is your carcass
pierced by the iron spike
of midnight.

VI. From *Dumuzi Mourned*

1.

Who was your mother?
I was your mother.
Who was your sister?
I was your sister.

Oh, my son-brother, Dumuzi.
Would God that the same dawn
dawned for the two of us.
each divided from the other.

2.

Who was his sister?
I was the sister of him
who blew life
through his five-stopped pipe.

Who was his mother?
I was the mother of him
who blew the truth,
the meadow-music
of the star-searching shepherds.

3.

How deeply you sleep, my son.
My brother, how deeply you sleep.
Your sleep is deeper
than the bedrocks of earth.

I cry to the hills,
"Where is my boy?"
I cry to the valleys,
"Where is my brother?

The hills answer,
"Nowhere that you may feed him."
The valleys echo,
"Nowhere that you may give him drink."

4.

Do you hear that piping?
It is my heart.
My heart is piping in the desert
the music of the mournful.
Do you hear that piping?
It is my soul.
My soul is piping in potter's fields
for him who, by the world, remains unsung.

5.

O Mother, the ax is laid
at the root of the tree.
O Sister, your brother has been felled.
Shorn of its branches is the hollow tree.

"Is it you?"
weeps the sister.
"Is it you?" the mother weeps.
"You have changed."

VII. From *The Son's Reply*

I cannot hear the desolated cry.
My ears are stopped.
Mud stops my ears.
I cannot hear the forlorning cry.

When the rain falls,
then sprouts the tender grass.
I am not rain.
I am not grass.

The vernal gardens fountain water.
Dry trees grow green again.
I am not water.
I am not trees.

I cannot hear
the long,
forsaken
cry.

VIII.

O Babylon!
Lock up! Lock up!
Lock your houses!
Lock your temples!

Say to the bride at the temple door,
"Abandon marriage.
Abandon love.
Abandon hope."

Walter Wangerin Jr.
December 21, 2016

53504705R00060

Made in the USA
San Bernardino, CA
18 September 2017